AFTER THE FLOOD

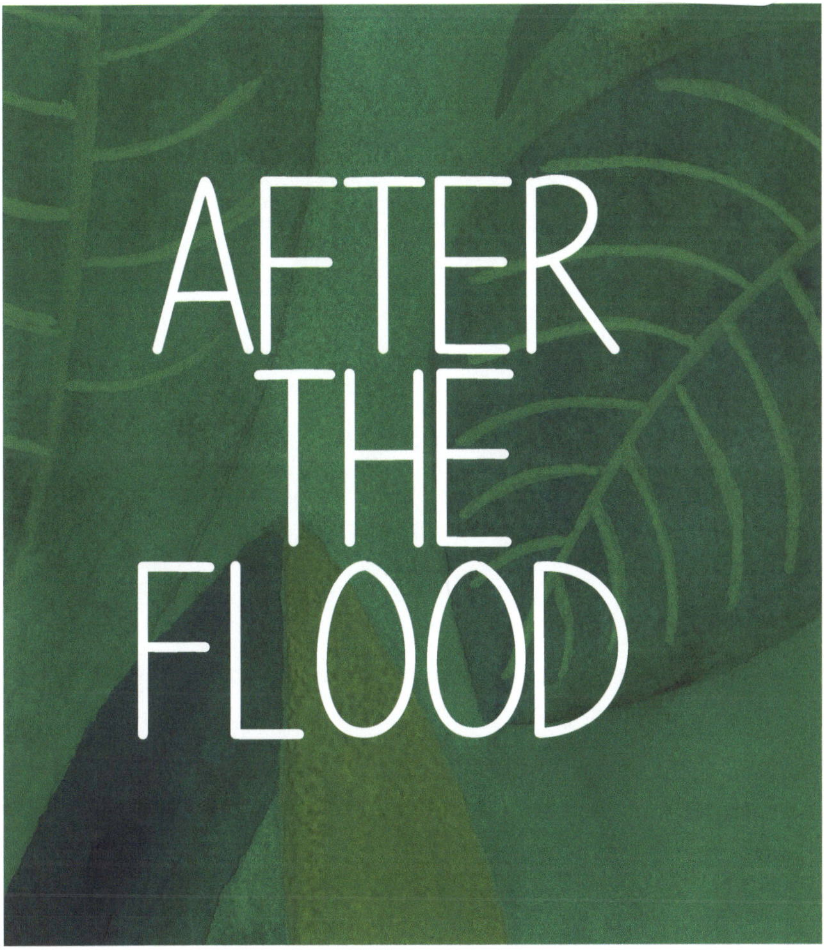

AFTER THE FLOOD
PAINTINGS BY GREG EDMONDSON

WRITINGS BY:

HELENE BARIL
JOHN DORSEY
GINA FERRARA
LINZI GARCIA
JONATHAN KLINE
JIM MCGOWIN
RC PATTERSON
NEZKA PFEIFER
JEANETTE POWERS
RUBEN QUESADA
STEFENE RUSSELL
BRETT UNDERWOOD
NADIA WOLNISTY

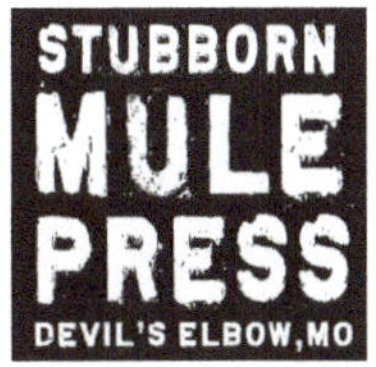

Stubborn Mule Press
Devil's Elbow, MO
stubbornmulepress.com

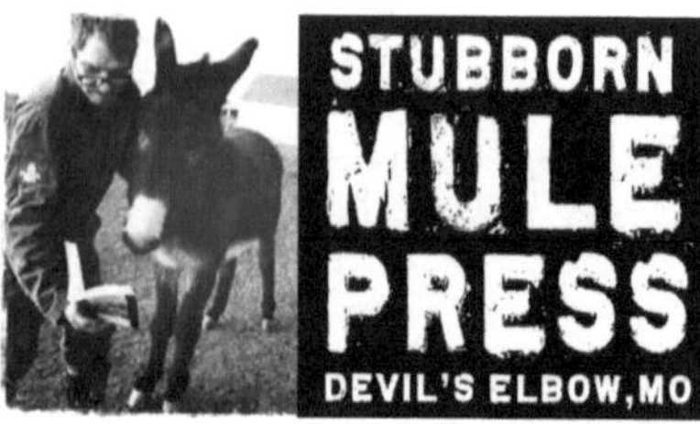

First Edition 11 7 5 3 2 1
ISBN: 978-1-950380-06-0
LCCN: 2019933166

Design, edits and layout: Jeanette Powers & Greg Edmondson
stubbornmulepress@gmail.com @stubbornmulepress
Cover Images: Greg Edmondson
All photos of artworks: Lisa Halley Melching

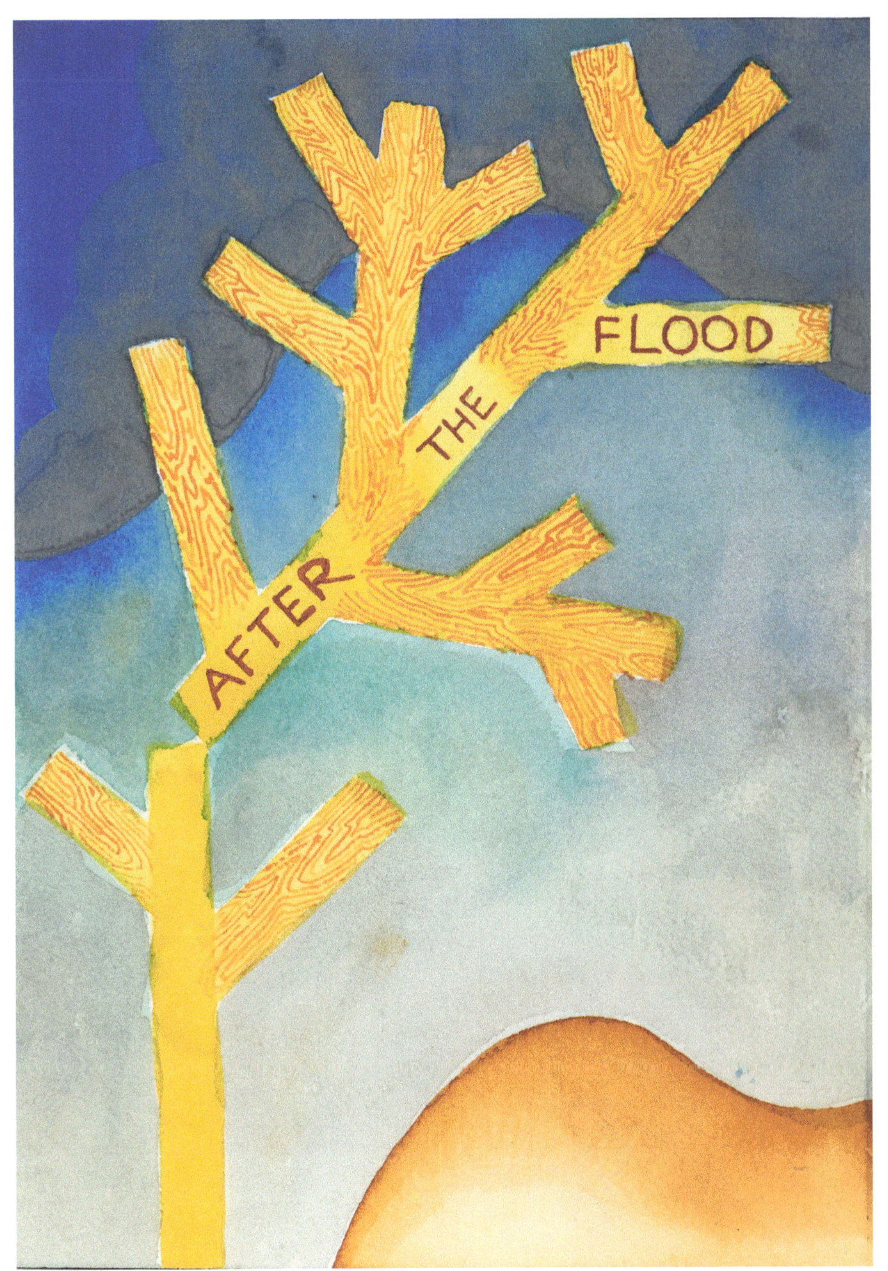

FLOOD
THE
AFTER

NOTE FROM THE PAINTER

This book is dedicated to all those who have taught me the hardest of lessons ...

The paintings collected in *After the Flood* were all made between October 2017 and October 2018, many in a single day. The book's title is both literal- in my 46 months on the Gasconade River she has flooded four times, twice requiring the evacuation of people and possessions, and twice requiring the couple who run the residency to spend 10 nights or so on a mattress in my studio while flood waters drained from their house; and figurative- I had spent the bulk of 2017 working on my first book of paintings, RIVERS and BEASTS. After submitting final edits to my publisher in September 2017, I returned to my studio feeling as if I'd washed ashore some place foreign or unfamiliar. All the finished works we'd photographed were put away and what remained were things abandoned. Scraps of ideas and unfinished thoughts littered the floor and the walls had been swept bare. I wasn't stuck, I could move, I could paint, but I was lost. I had no map or no compass to tell me which direction was "forward". I began making these little watercolors as a way of finding my way again.

Utmost thanks to Lisa Halley Melching who photographed the works collected here and nearly everything I've made in the past four years.

—Greg Edmondson, January, 2019

INTRODUCTION

The first thing that excited me about Greg's work when I first saw it years ago, was his inspired use of patterns, taking a mundane human-made artifact and painting a layer of another pattern on top, creating a surprising and unique work that was much more than the sum of its parts. He recenters an aesthetic narrative, making us adjust and see new stories to items we didn't think possible.

He has continued to make work since that time using patterns to highlight the world he observes, whether it's in natural surroundings or human-made environments. And now he's done it again. *AFTER THE FLOOD* explores the world he's inhabited for a few years near the Gasconade River in Missouri, taking the palimpsests of what remained after the many times the waters receded and using his unique perspective to create new work to rise above the floodwaters.

Greg's use of color is electric. The works here are bright, arresting, and forge new paths for him. His painted lines capture the mathematics of nature, with beautiful proportions. And he sees the essential grooves that we see in trees, and leaves, and twigs, and rivulets; he paints for us to look at them and notice them more closely. Greg is an artist who makes us look to see the small things and understand that their beauty is constant and ever present.

The paintings also confirm Greg's mastery of watercolor, the toughest of media. The precision of his brush seems to carve the lines into the paper, and yet the translucency of this liquid medium give an openness and space to what could so easily become rigid and ossified. The spectrum of colors change with the range of techniques Greg uses, whether he's painting abstractly, or a finely detailed work of art.

AFTER THE FLOOD presents the work of an artist at a crossroads in time, but not in talent.

—Nezka Pfeifer, Museum Curator,
Stephen and Peter Sachs
Museum, Missouri Botanical
Garden, St. Louis, MO

FIRST OF OCTOBER

GOUACHE ON PAPER, 10" X 7"

2017

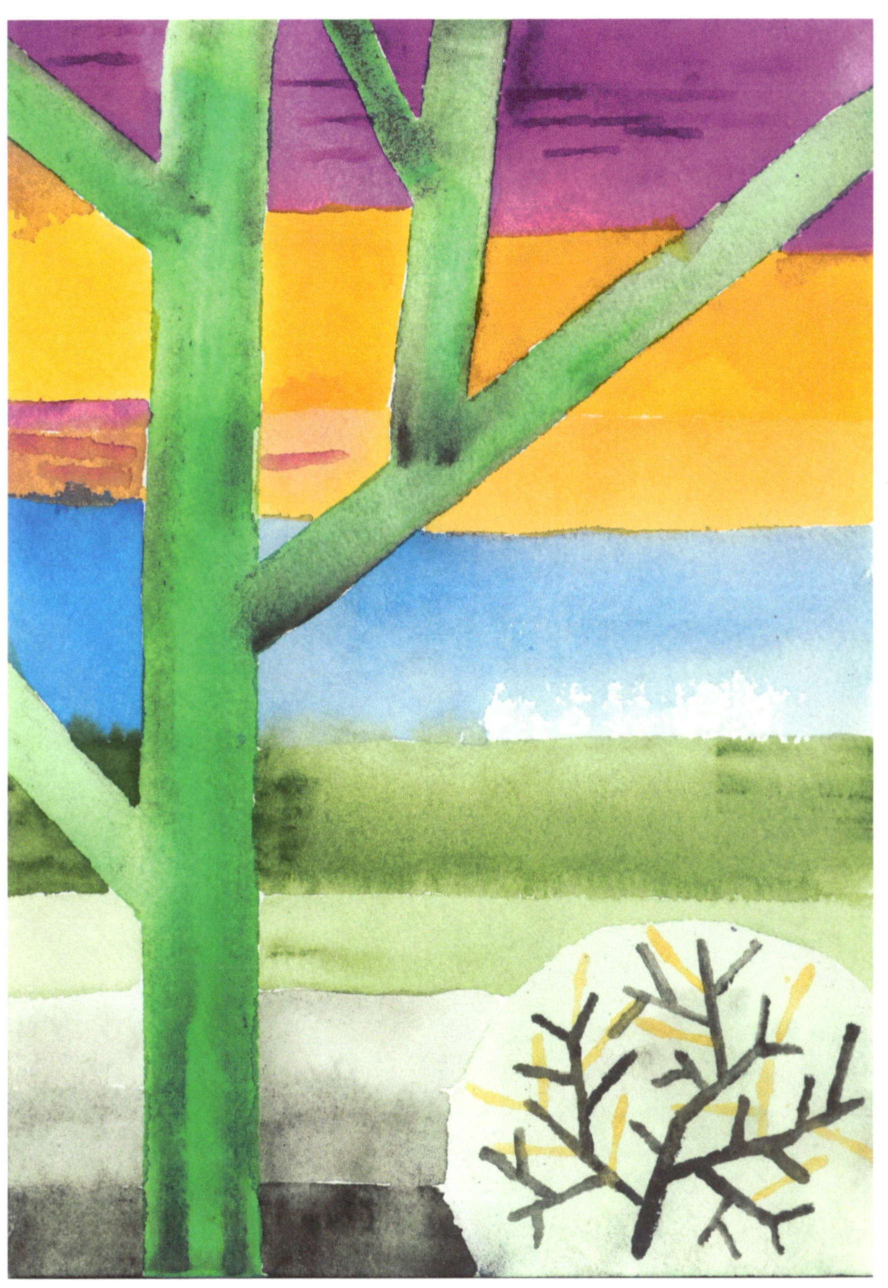

PROUD LITTLE PEACOCK
OR, NO FOOL LIKE AN OLD FOOL

GOUACHE ON PAPER, 10" X 7"
2017

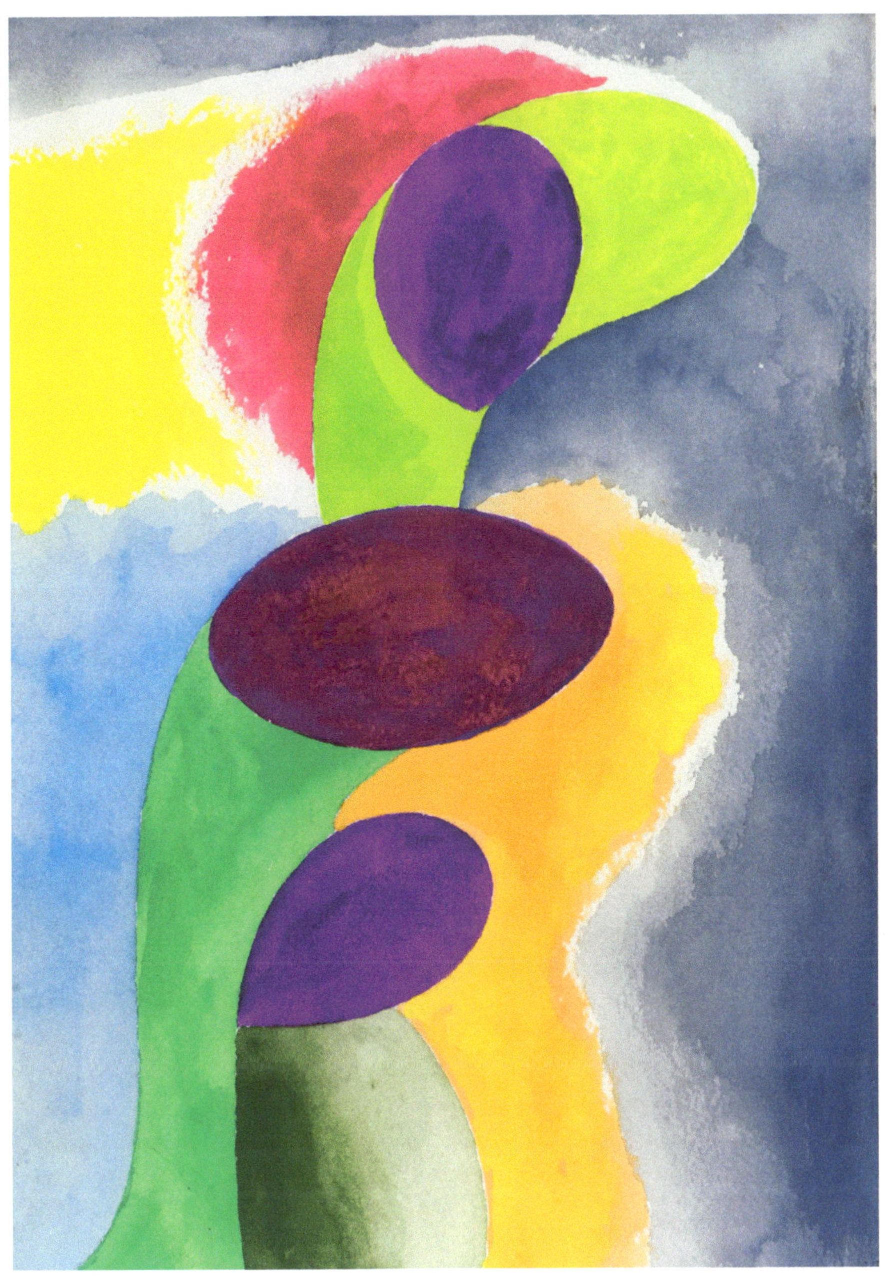

SPEAKEASY

GOUACHE ON PAPER, 10" X 7"
2017

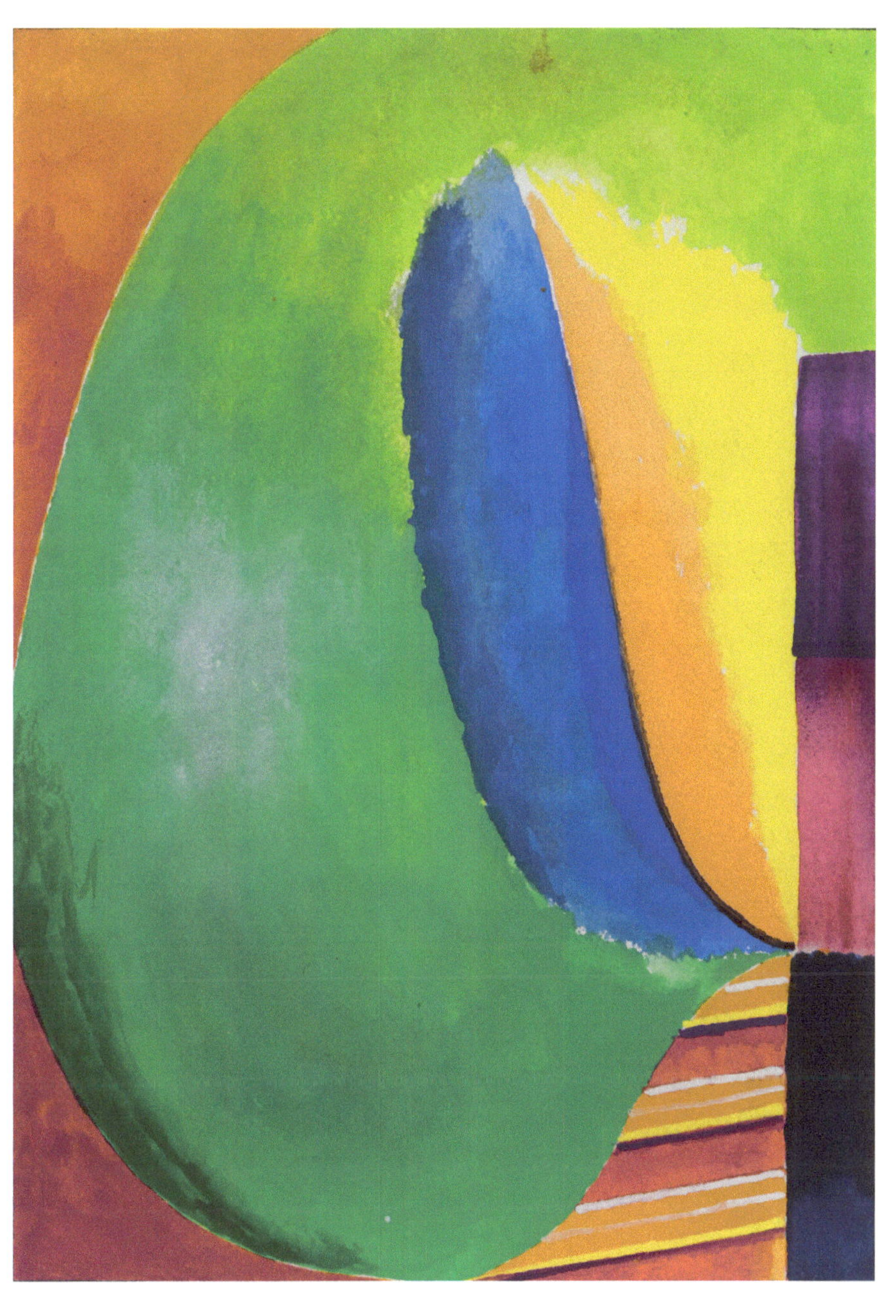

STORM WARNING

GOUACHE ON PAPER, 10″ X 7″

2017

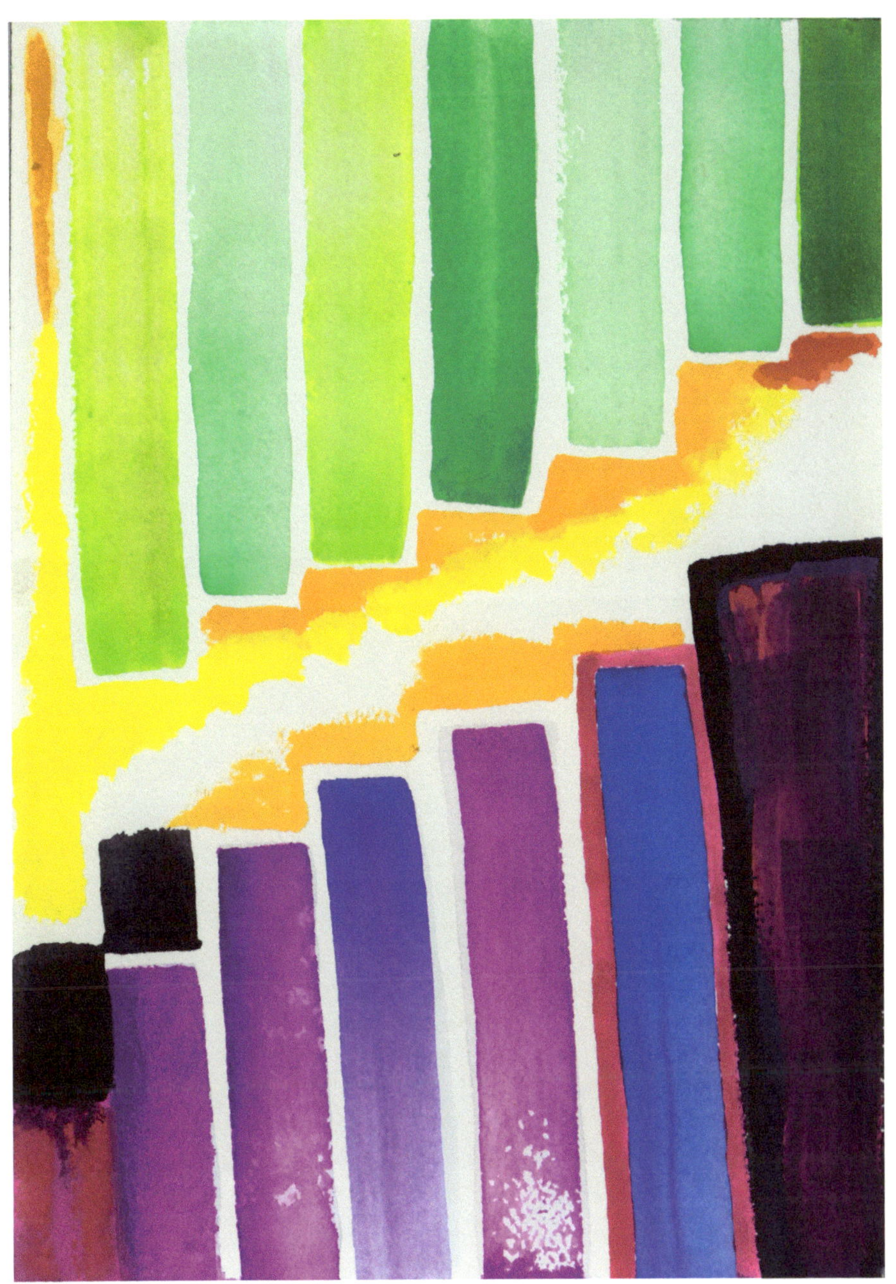

WINDFALL
GOUACHE ON PAPER, 10" X 7"
2017

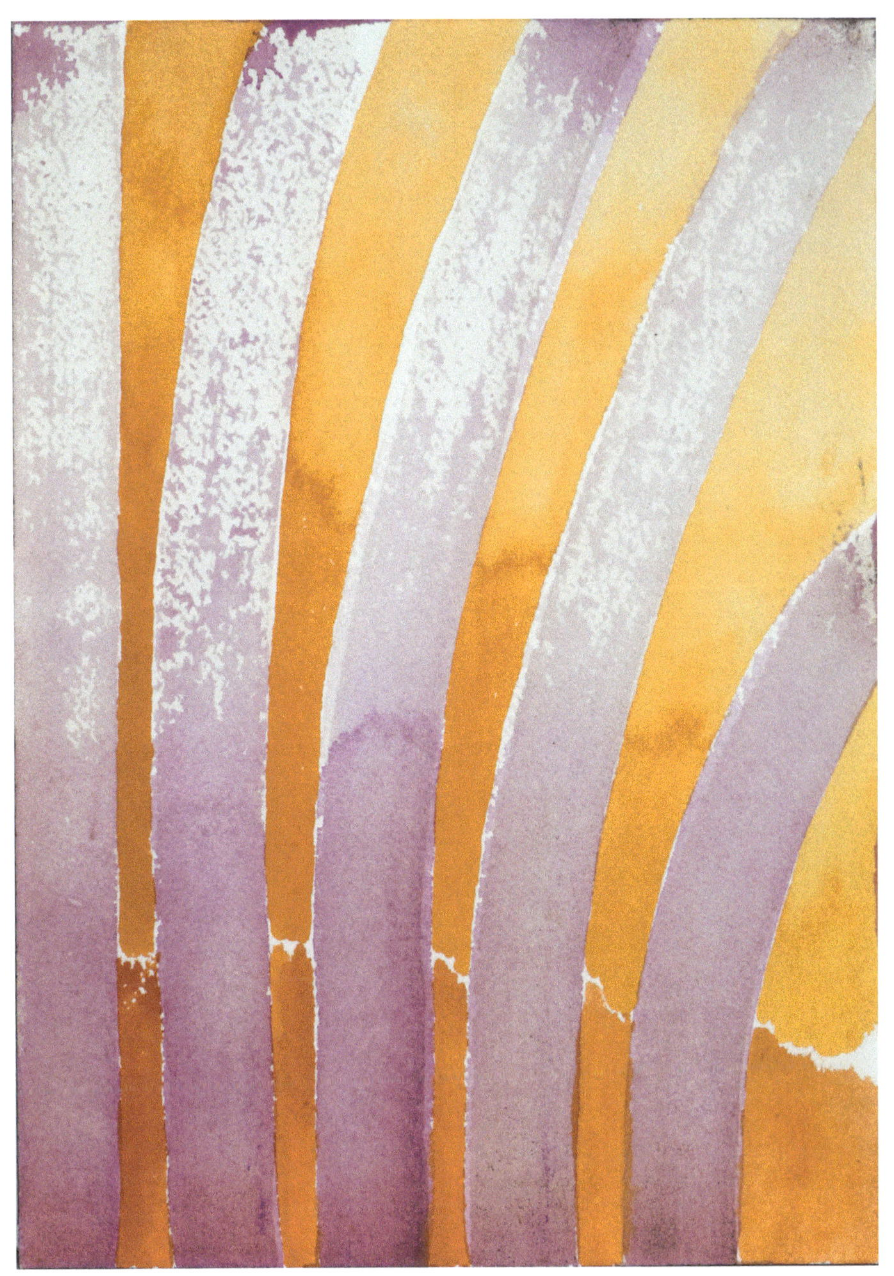

CLEAN SWEEP

GOUACHE ON PAPER, 10" X 7"

2017

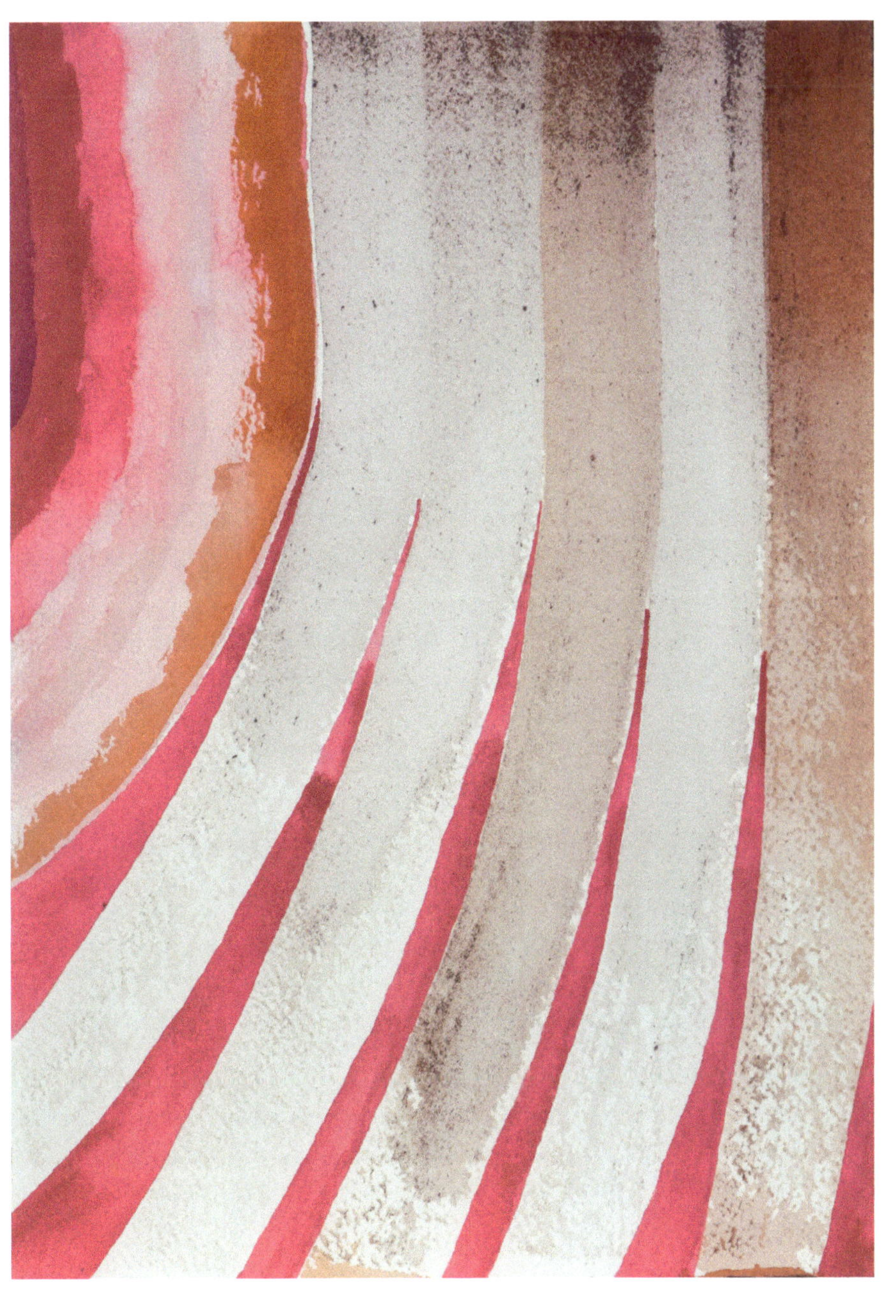

BRUSH FIRE
GOUACHE ON PAPER, 10" X 7"
2018

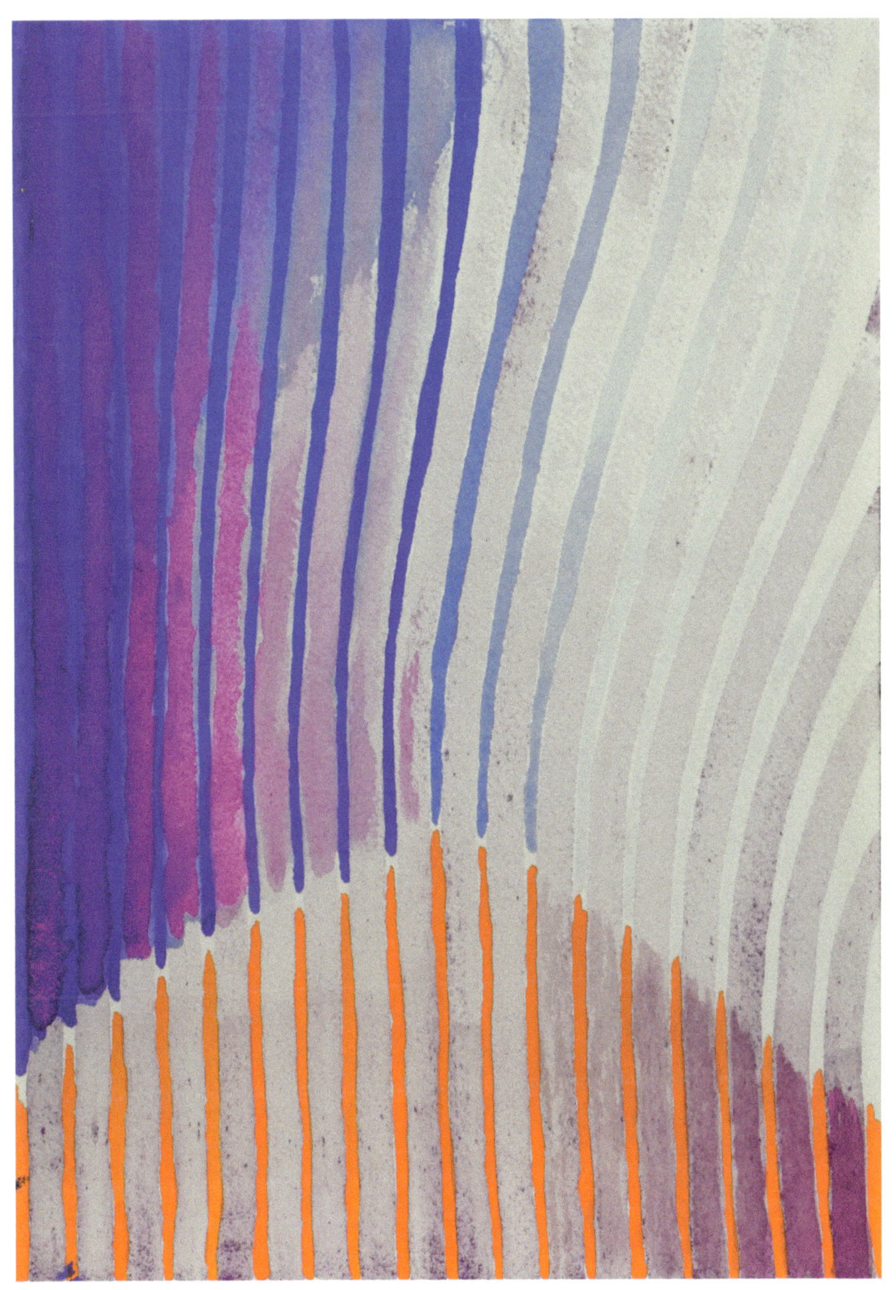

A SINGLE RAY OF LIGHT

GOUACHE ON PAPER, 10" X 7"

2018

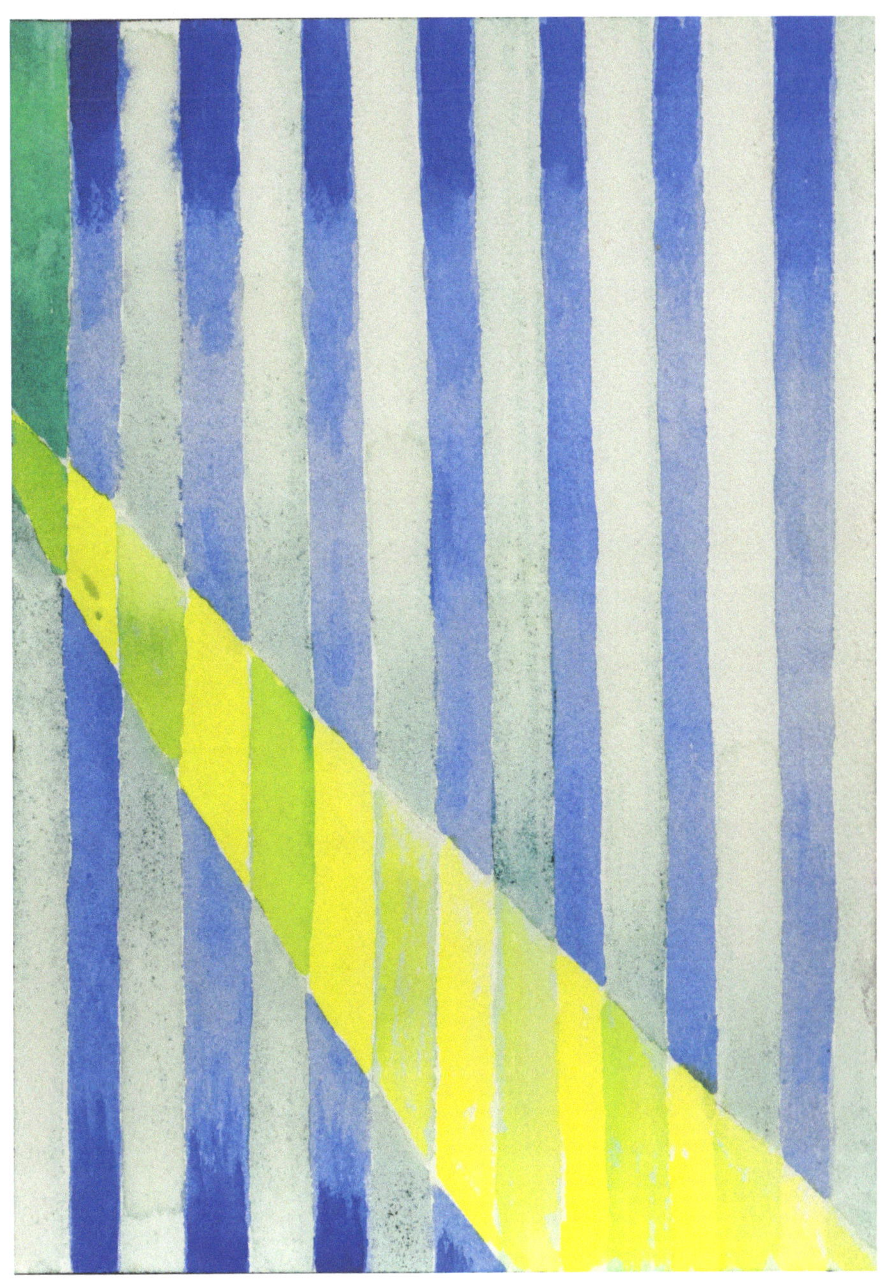

ECHO CHAMBER
OR, SHADOW OF A DOUBT
GOUACHE ON PAPER, 10" X 7"
2018

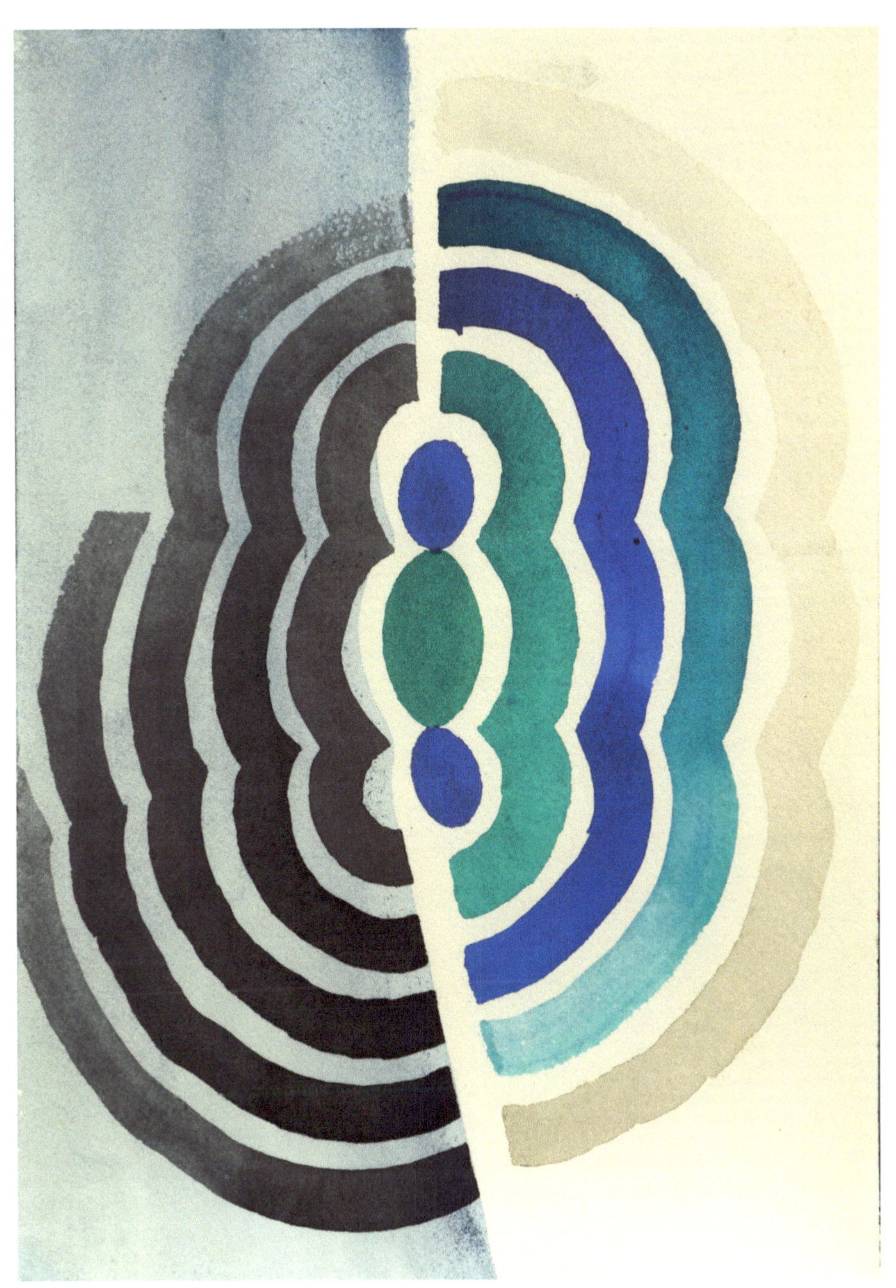

SNAKE GRASS
GOUACHE ON PAPER, 10" X 7"
2018

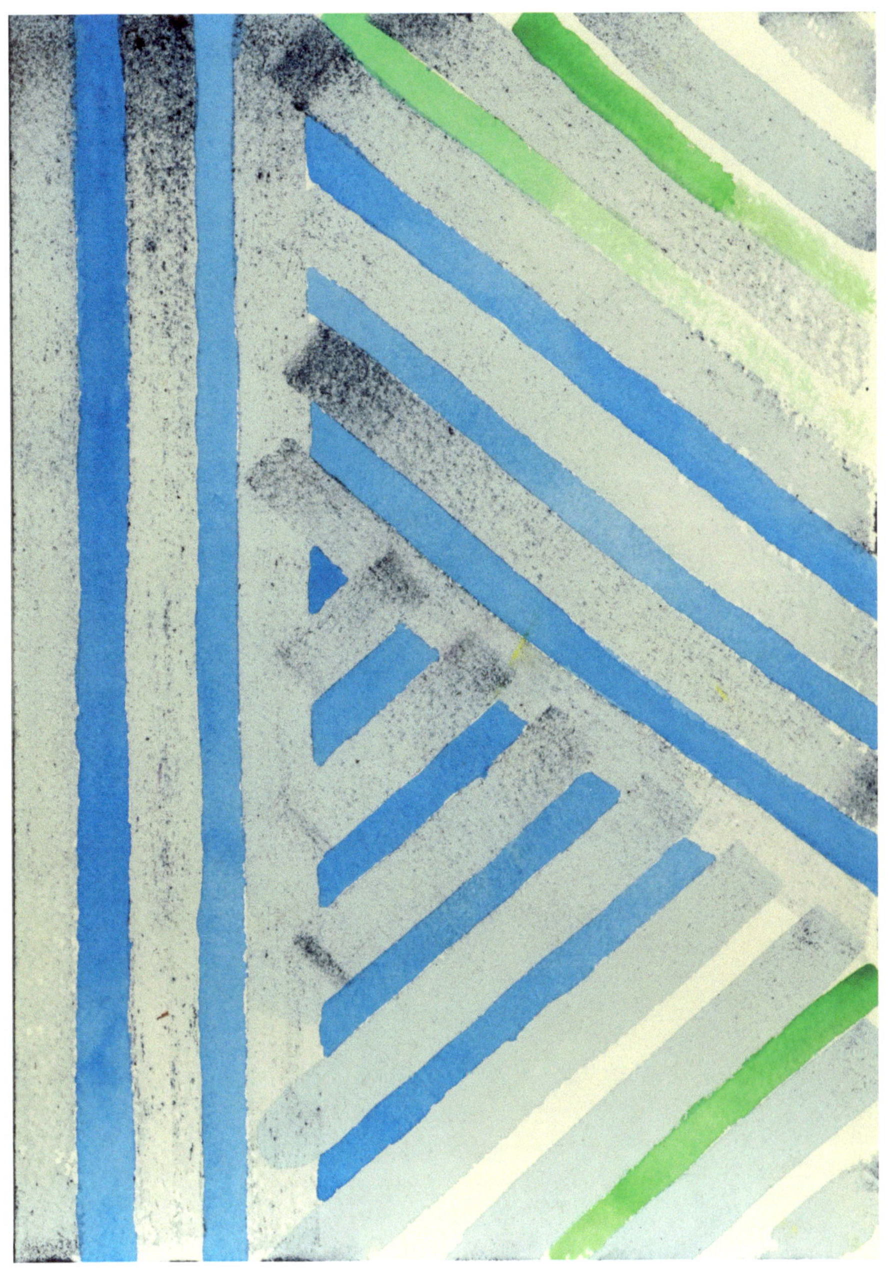

ROCK CLIMBING

GOUACHE ON PAPER, 9" X 6"

2018

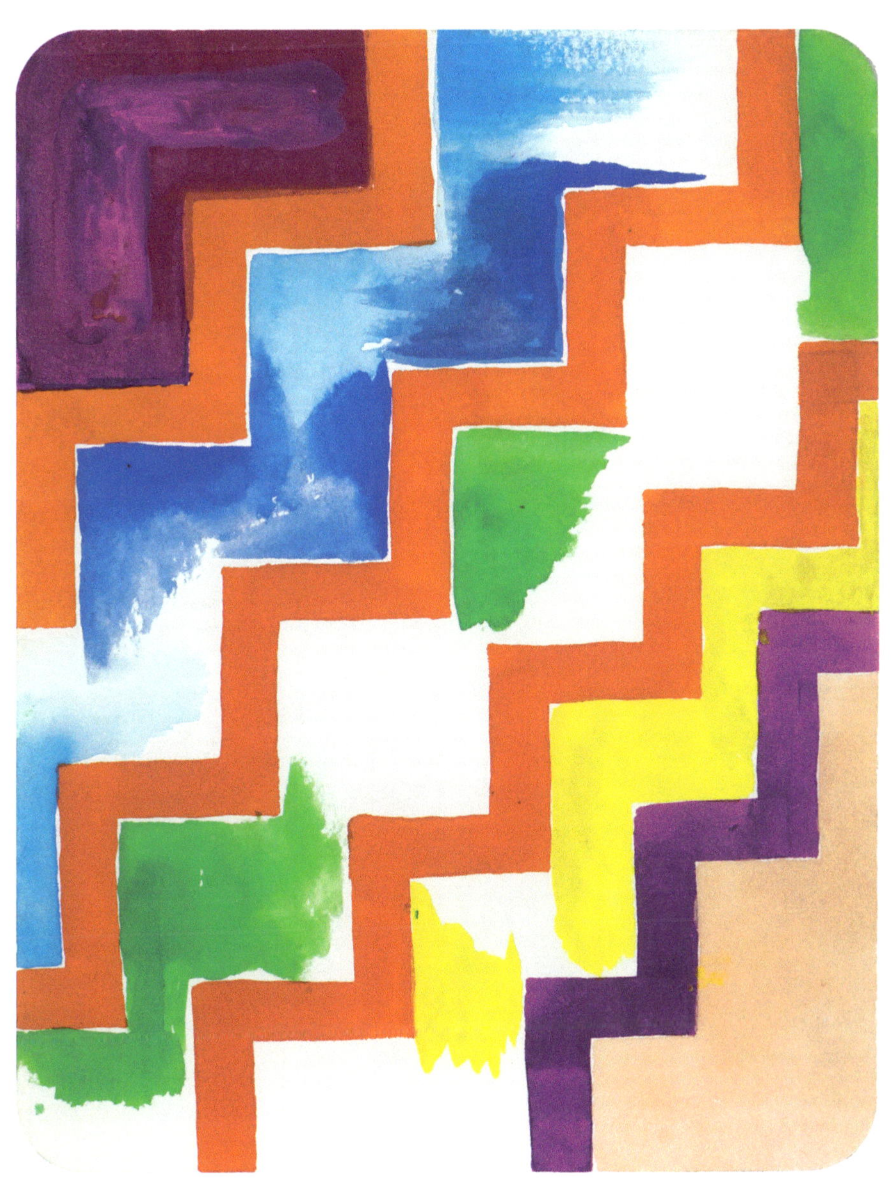

THE ELEPHANT IN THE ROOM

GOUACHE ON PAPER, 9" X 6"

2018

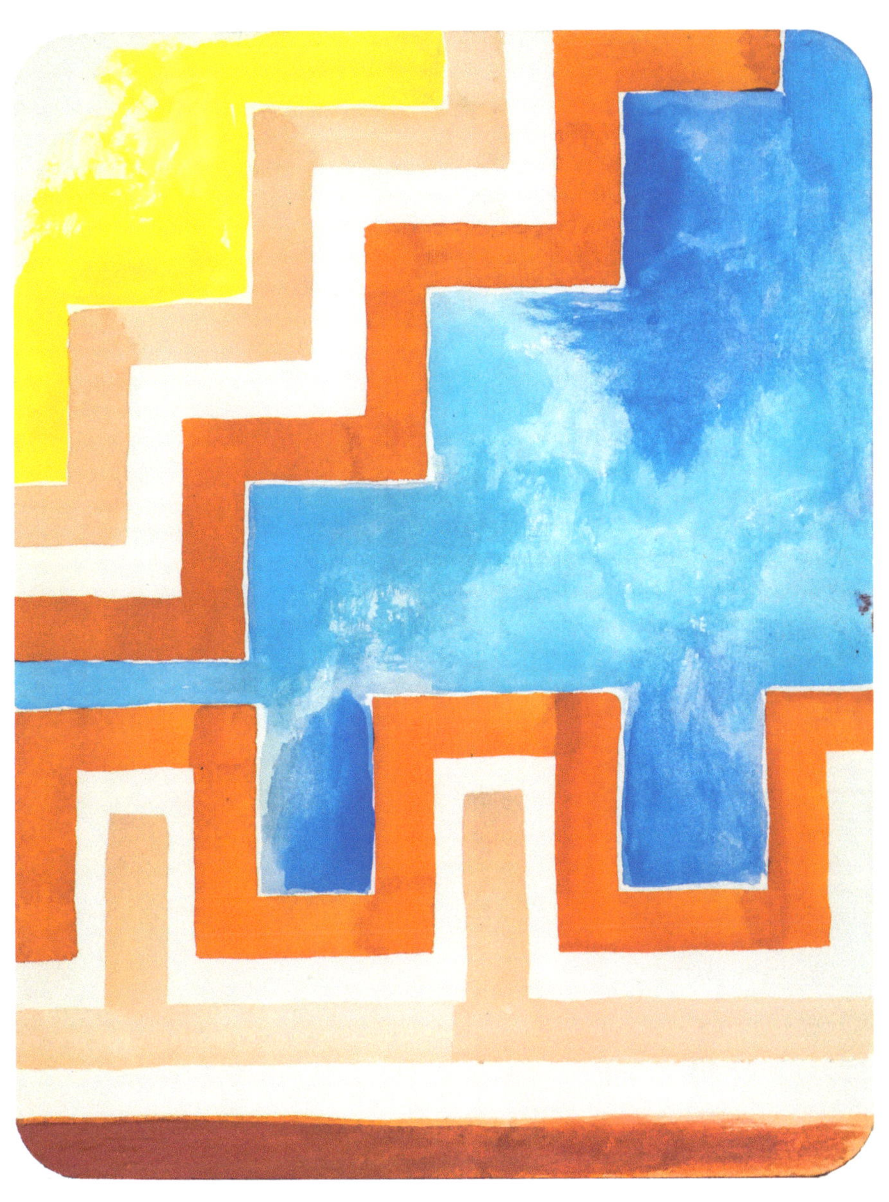

JULY
GOUACHE on PAPER, 10" X 7"
2018

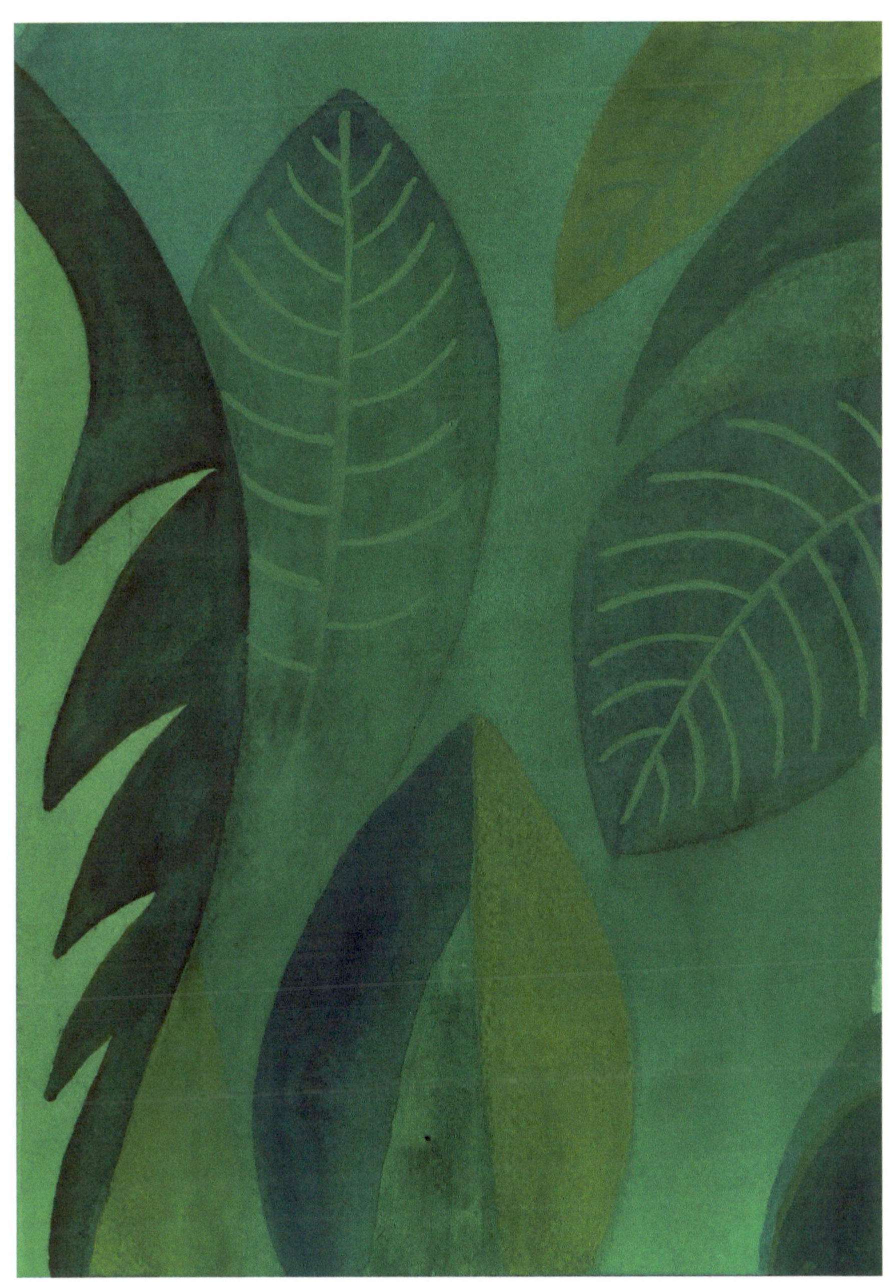

THREE DEAD TREES
GOUACHE ON PAPER, 10" X 7"
2018

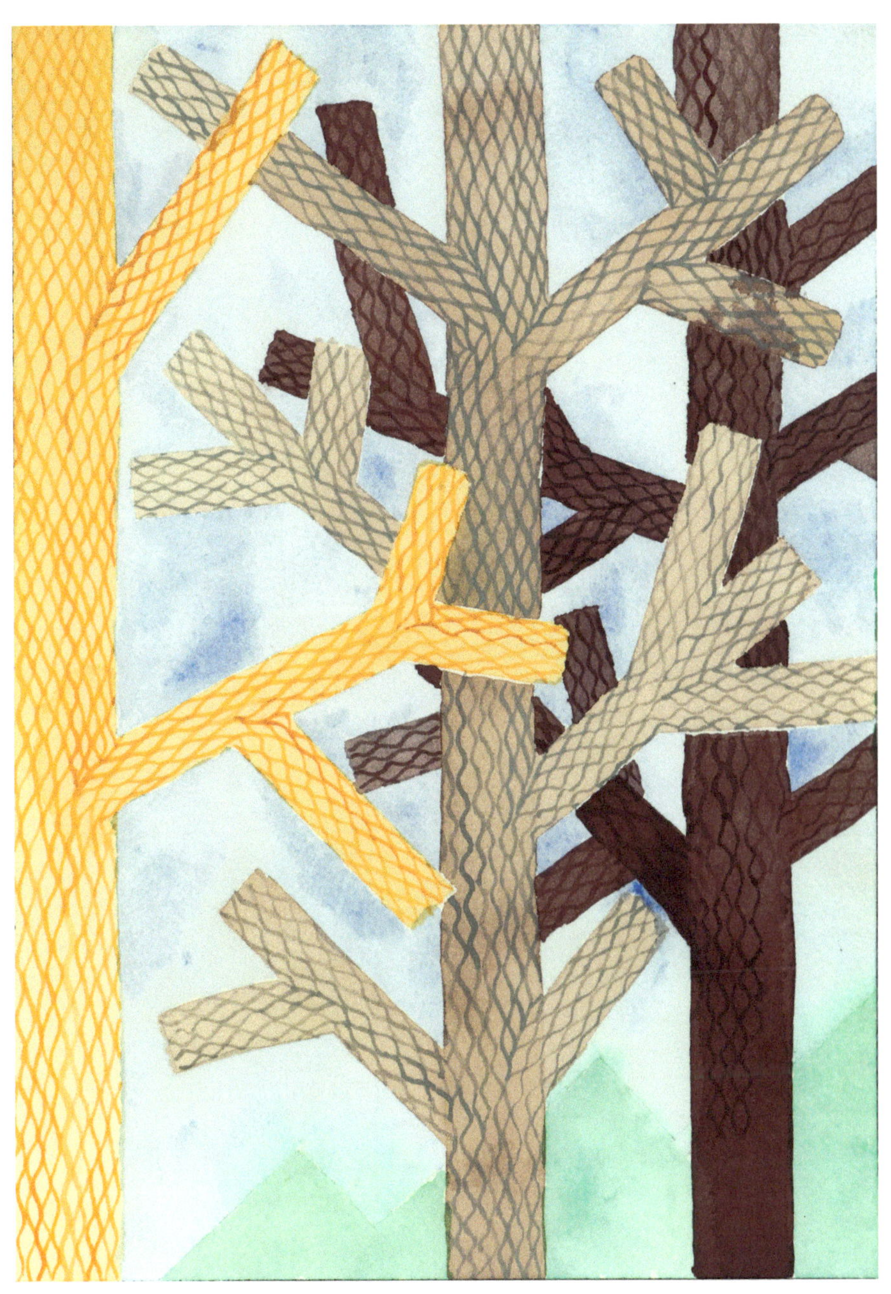

SKELETON KEY
GOUACHE ON PAPER, 10" X 7"
2018

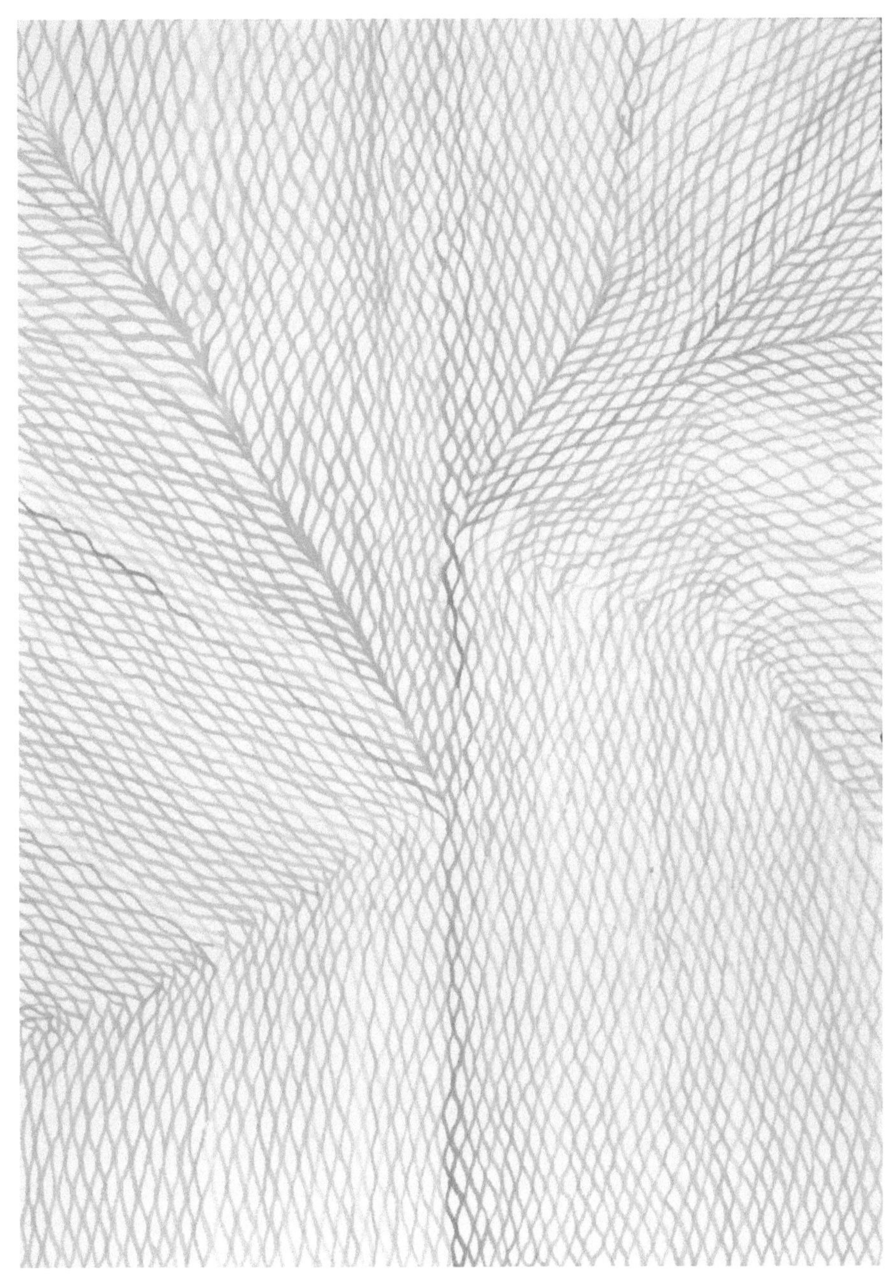

OCTOBER AGAIN
GOUACHE ON PAPER, 10" X 7"
2018

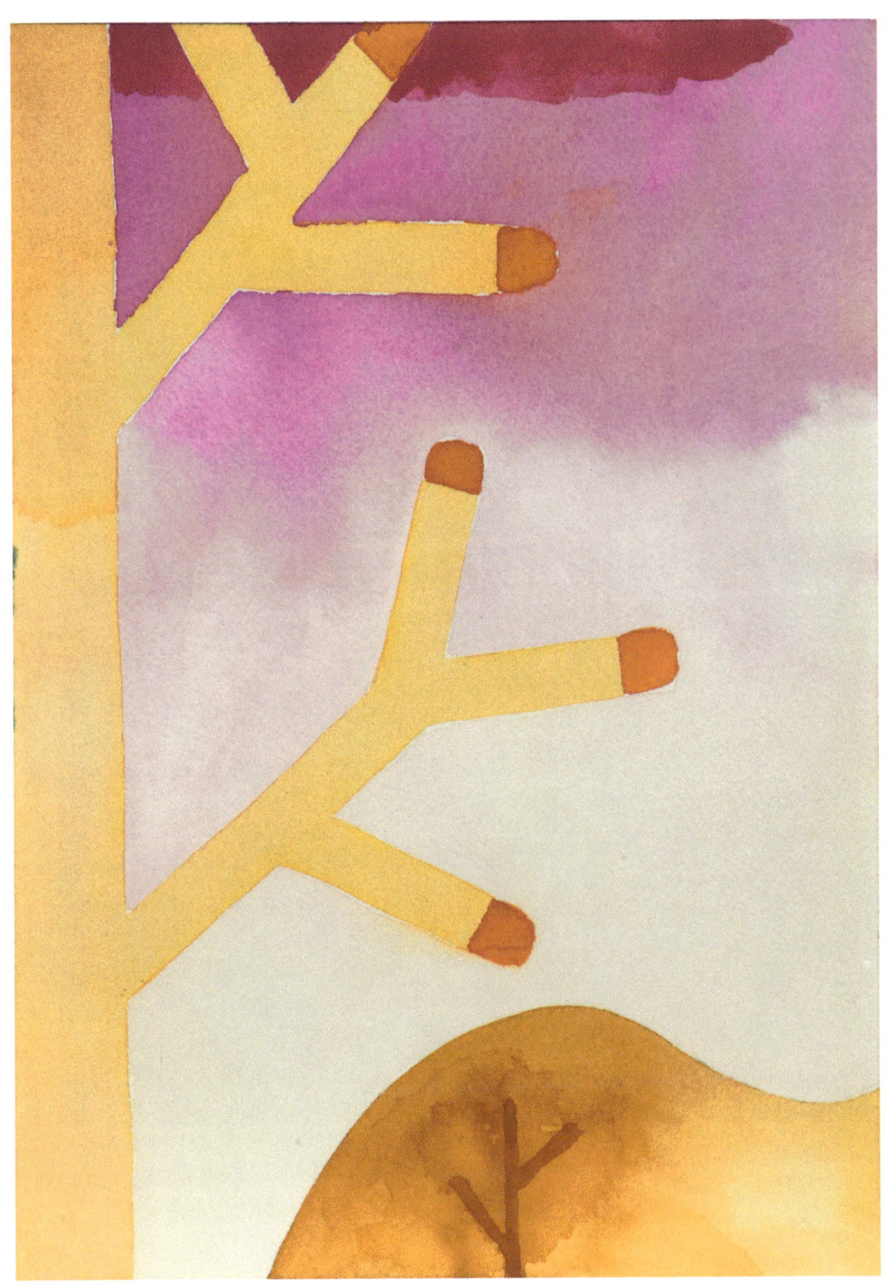

WRITINGS

After the Flood

we are all pinned down in one room
& heather has tony trying
to connect to the internet for hours
so she can watch
the latest episode of sherlock

she may be revolutionizing
the american theater
or whipping cream
into pure hate

but she doesn't have a clue
about common courtesy
that some telescopes can see
into the human heart

or that true revolution
comes from within.

"AFTER THE FLOOD"

Nine Months After The Storm

In that first early summer after the storm
sunflowers hung their heads like skinny prom dates
as the city counted my neighbors husband among the dead
flood sown pumpkin seeds
swelled across her lawn
out to the sidewalk up
over the nailed shut door
acid green valentines quilting in the dry slime
long white blossoms in the gray mat grass
Then the pregnant pumpkins grew
1 pound
3 pound
5 pound 10
fat sallow bellies full of flood
2 doors down
Al the cop put them on his porch
dreaming of Katrina pies
and the severed heads of looters
I came home one night and all the vines were gone
 Al just stood over the heap of hearts and blossoms
shining his flash light
as if the work had been done by vandals
"Looka dis..." he said
"all dem baby punkins"

"FIRST OF OCTOBER"

i want a mad fall in love story- mutual

Are you serious? because I've got a shitload to unload!!!!!!
I want people to start being FUCKING HONEST about
their BAD behavior and how it affects/effect the very
people they claim to care about!

i know i'm supposed to assume that if i meet enough
assholes, the problem is really me, and that it's
problematic if everyone i trust has known me less than a
year...but to be honest, i think i'm the exception, and all
of the people i've surrounded myself with prior to now
were all just assholes by coincidence.

My boss set up a one on one quick meeting tomorrow
and I have no idea what to discuss and it freaks me out.

Prepare for war. Assume that he has it out for you and
you need to tell him, point-by-point, why he's a shit boss.
If you're wrong and its something mundane, you won't
regret it. If the anxiety is correct, you won't have any
regrets.

My dad was a pretty awful guy.

All I've wanted for the last 10 years is to get married,
have (a) kid(s), and make an early-retirement/vacation
plan, but nobody wants to do the second part so

It's been a year since I've been intimate with another.
Almost 3 years since I've had a committed partner. And
though I am a creature of partnership, this is the most..
in my Self, and loving that Self, I have ever been.. and I
feel(fear) it'll be this...<u>SEE MORE</u>

Nuance is dead. All is transparent now. Humanity has

reached its zenith. It's all down from here, and that's okay too. We are learning to love ourselves again.

OH fUCK OK....MEN AND WOMEN WHO LIKE TO TALK ABOUT PHYSICALLY FIGHTING PEOPLE ARE LAME? AND I ASSUME THEY ARE STUPID THE MOMENT ANY HINT OR INUENDO OF THAT COMES OUT OF THEIR MOUTH ....FOREST GUMP AND THE ENTIRE CULTURE OF THE 90S IS OVERRATED....I'M ALSO MAD AT MY DAD FOR DIVORCING MY MOM IN 1988 AND ALSO AT MY MOM?

My family's political views frighten me

Like
Reply

Your comment here...

BOTTOM OF FORM

The Give and Go

Did you know?
The expeditor was talking to the gumbo
and wouldn't listen to the wisdom
of the andouille when dialysis landed
on the fish ballot.

The chuckleheads took it
as a clue to ignore.
Given their dos and don'ts;
their wills and wont's
and what comes with the donuts
and coffee, they had to question
the regularity of the clouds' offerings.

The diners were oblivious
as the osprey with the arrow in its throat cried.
The give and go.
You came and you went.
You go along. You get along.

But sometimes
you gotta exclaim,
"What?!!!"

"SPEAKEASY"

Insidious

Riding this bus feeling grain on the threshing floor of a Popeye's in a North City Fleamarket where me and a friend bought boot leg music and movies. All roads lead to *Aufhebung.*

That night as we watched Insidious we noticed a stranger pissing right outside the window. This stranger looked at us and smiled.

"STORM WARNING"

Newton's Second Law

I used to do a lot of things without you
like dancing in the living room
and making three-course meals
with just one plate, one candle,
one Moon.

I'd watch the clouds hide
and think of you being hidden too
sometimes it was as though
a single day took a lifetime
but then suddenly months and years
were gone before a single dish was done
and it felt like all the songs were over
like all the music was gone
and I held absolutely still
no pressure, no motion, no me.

Because without you is a hollow
is an aperture with no end
waiting for you
I am less than a wisp
I am currentless
I can't even be detected
because without you
there is only absence.

"WINDFALL"

Respire

Fragile gardenia.
Any scent of paradise is lost.
Now the leaves are black,
marked with pocks in patterns
that are the antithesis of constellations,
closer to cancerous
as dreaded spots on lungs.

These are real just like the pebble sized
spot that appeared on the x-ray.
Blind-sided. Ripples made
the rocks waver.

You gave up cigarettes forever,
the habitual inhaling and exhaling
gray white smoke in solitary letters
hanging ampersands and lurid rings,
the last unfiltered pack
crumpled into submission
so that your lungs might expand
to the size of what happens next.

"CLEAN SWEEP"

Disruption

Water creeps
     through earth,
     cutting the land's edges,
     peeling Missouri's skin.

 A raw,
     saturated silt underbelly
is scraped to the surface.

It understands disruption,
impermanence.

"BRUSH FIRE"

Destination

Green, yellow, brown, bright,
Sure.
I miss the terribly, beautiful
Sunsets.
Red, orange steaming heat
Yeah.
That's part of it.
Breezes and bicycles
Flowing skirts and leaves blowing
Hot dogs and horses
All right.

But I like the gray
The monochromatic
and the subtle hints.
And I know that all those
colors are captured in the one
The white light.
I like the magic in a
screaming snowball
in the night
All the colors in that jagged
orb.
That is where I am headed.
That glaring sunlight
of one circle
The gross of pain and love.
Take me there.

"A SINGLE RAY OF LIGHT"

Shadow of a Doubt

And when the song said that even the sun sets on paradise
I thought of you then my body broke into mist
forming a colorless cloud —dear friend—
who once laughed and wept and now
the only thing left is darkness. I remember
sitting in the next room and hearing the low slow note
of your exhale as you slept like an oboe's mumble
through house. I've heard this music each night.
I never imagined the music the body makes
could charm me. This poem is not about you—
why should it have any purpose beyond knowing
it exists. Don't go into the light. Let the light in you
eclipse your own sorrow—break break break—
you are already a garden in the sky.

"ECHO CHAMBER"

Time is an Electronic River

Acknowledgement:
Lyn Hejinian, Ursula K. Le
Guin, Octavia E. Butler and my
friends the she poets living in
Paris

I am a she dog that sees ghosts
I met a poet she was from Kansas City
I met her in the town I have been hunting for
And where I live now – Kagis –
All the cities of the world start with a K
Since the flood
The poet, I think she could not figure out what I was
She had never seen a dog before
I inspired her
Time is an electronic river
She writes
I am a she dog that sees ghosts
I have come where I was going
I found, at least, the city I had been hunting for
I invented a city and I called it Kagis
The only other human people in my family
Live on the islands
Time is an electronic river
She had been lonely
Since she realized
She would not die like other people
They would always leave her
But I can see them
I am a she dog that sees ghosts
I invented a city and I called it Kagis
I live there with the poet

I see ghosts, she writes
I talk to her dead relatives
And tell her about their stories
Time is an electronic river

59

"SNAKE GRASS"

Snake Grass

Sneak Grass, crawling like dodder.
Snipe Grass, just try to find it.
Ache Grass, jointed and pointy.
Switch Grass, shifty and fuzzy.
Bear Grass, clover for sleeping.
Cheat Grass, too short for mowing.
Needle Grass, good for cursing.
Freak Grass, blue and shaking.
Nun Grass, grey and blushing.
Panic Grass, ripe for the reaping.
Barnyard Grass, purple and bristly.
Jiminy Grass, cousin of Timothy.
Crown Grass, blades undefeated.
Vinegar Grass, Rx for weeping.
Snake Grass, turf of Abraxas.

"SNAKE GRASS"

Jim McGowin

Potnia Theron in Snakes of Blue & Green

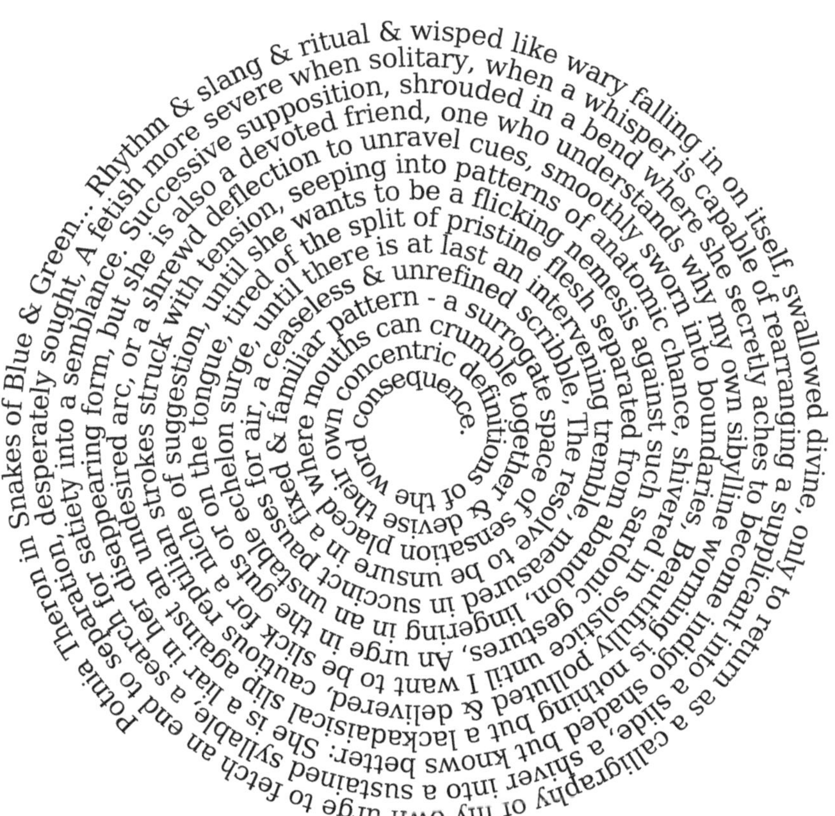

"SNAKE GRASS"

You Would Start a Fight at a Hospital, and I Love You for It, but That's Not What I Need Right Now

I prefer my grief to come in installments.
No quick bursts, no fall down the stairs.
Grief does not even have to come regularly,
like daily mail you have to open with your silver
letter opener to avoid cuts, or the blood-knowledge
you are not pregnant.
A different type of moon-cycle when
it comes in the daytime. There, there
is your grief—cold balloon staring.
Why here, and why today? No rhythm
to it. Have you ever gone rock-climbing.
Each movement is staccato and swing.
No one sees you but the moon,
if there is a moon in the daytime.
Look down and your hands are full of blood.

Stress Less (or a lightness of vision)

The almost.
I've got it.
The almost will take the
game most nights.
I'll have another
Then wish I was somewhere
someone else.
No slaphappy dingaling.

It is inevitable.
I know it.
Still,
there's no one to
stop it.
No mopeydope can.
It is hope which tosses
such feelings aside.
Only hope.
We must hope for a better
tomorrow as
human beings...or else.

Or else what?

One will say,
"Hope is a crutch."
Hope is an anomaly.
Hope for less ennui.

Then why?
If why,
then how?

An epiphany:
Stress kills.
So don't worry.
Stop watching.
Stop sucking at
the glass tit of fear.

Do.
Listen and act.
That is it.

Blue Revolution

"JULY"

The pool is the sky and the sky is cerulean. The boarder of the pool is lightening. To get to the cerulean one must cross lightening. Only people made of lines can dive into the pool.

Rippling, fluctuating, these people of line live in a world defining the cerulean. The center was the cerulean until the people of lines overthrew the sky. Now the sky rules and the people of the line can haunt the cerulean pool as the center.

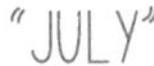

Faith

She saw a dog puppet licking the branch
                              outside her window
She had 17 girly, vodka drinks and a bottle of wine
painted naked in acrylic all night long
Later that afternoon the dog puppet
dissolved into pain

"THREE DEAD TREES"

Metatron or Marmaton

I am so small

& have to choose the
cordgrass six feet tall

over eyelashes turned to
flashes of lightning

& the hydrograph
over Enoch's fiery monograph

my road is water:
the marmot river
& the lazy Mare D'Zeen

voygeuse whose bones
will never glow like
sticks of burning juniper

or speak in alphabets
traced by burning stars

it's enough
to cross the water
here

on a rusted truss revealed
by leafless trees

"SKELETON KEY"

At 59

greg talks about wasted years
and missed opportunities

"they used to pop up
like the sunrise," he says
sipping a flat beer
on his porch
in middle of winter
in missouri

in his head
he is a young man
watching the berlin wall go down
on a busted black and white tv
imagining the future
while searching for bones
to place on canvas
in the rubble

he crushes a dead leaf
scattering its ashes
in the snow

"summer will be here
before we know it," he says

and the sun
will be blood red
with redemption.

This last painting is the first in the idea for the book you
are now holding. Jim McGowin wrote *The Prescription
for Burning* as a response to the painting *Prescribed
Burn* in early 2018. The conversations which
ensued were the initial kernal of ideas
which allowed this collaboration
to grow and take form.

PRESCRIBED BURN
ACRYLIC & GOUACHE ON LINEN, 20" X 16"
2017

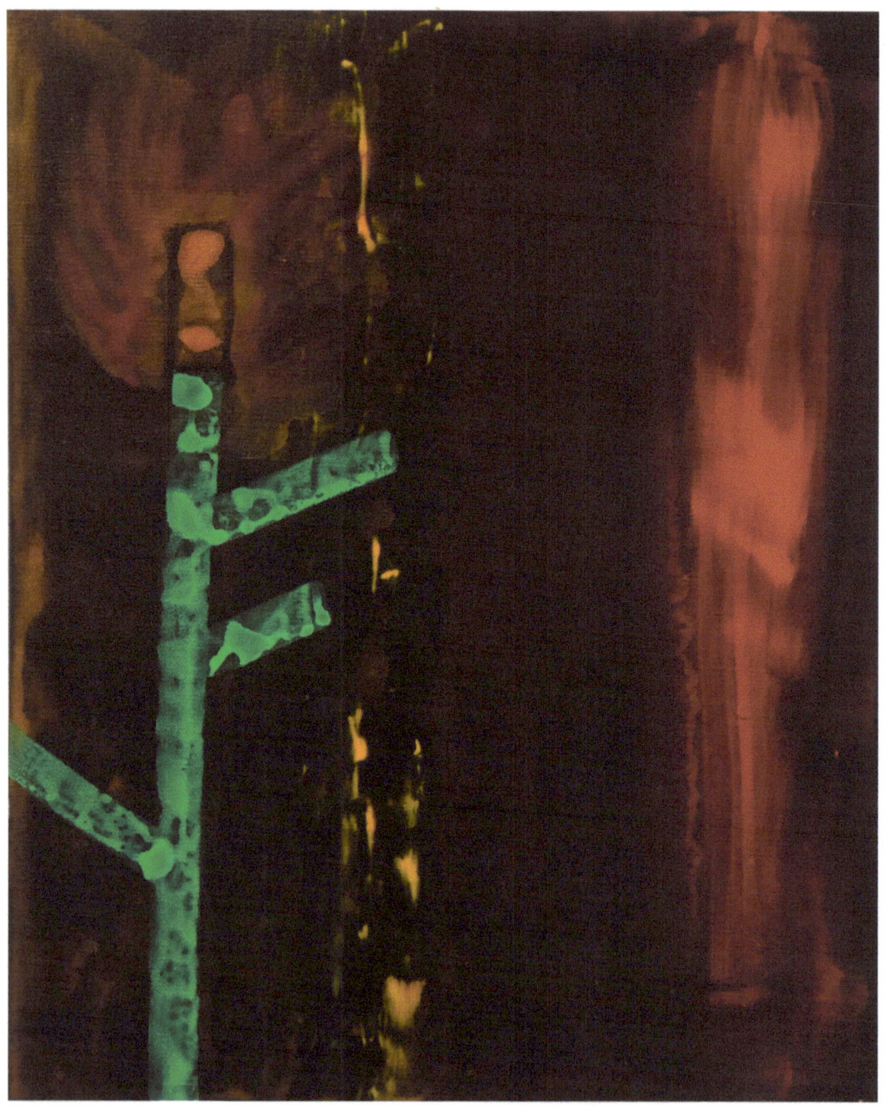

The Prescription for Burning

The afternoon is a determined, shadowy umber,
so burn it the rest of the way into a blackness
& declare it illuminated, if only by touch.

Onto a coarse cloth, lay down your conscience,
a benevolent measure,
assured & surrendered by the hand in
that obscure way of
holding onto the meaning, if only by a thread,
& redirecting it to spell out in a single glyph -
the devotion of budding aspiration.

What the hand puts down in casual strokes
the eye can only dream about confessing -
an absolute wounded tower
hidden in a spare green sprig,
ignited with red medicine.

Who would ask to be so illuminated,
just a kiss beyond the darkness?
The stain of single hewn captivation
versus a destructive way of saying,
a beholding in the incident,
intimidating like a prayer,

A prayer to know the color of a female form
so well
that she disappears into the past,
spoken in a syllable
so thin
it can only be streaked with memory,
so deep

that the intention is
slashed & declared complete
in a vague stroke of dusk-shimmered mercy,

And an oath that all the lit embers on
those tobacco colored nights wouldn't burn you,
as you vented negation with bare breath
back into the unseen sky,
knowing that the wind, it was not.

Cutting the night off, declaring the injured,
& asking to take a moment
just to smolder & hold to your inspiration,

Because breathing it all back out too willingly
would only inflict a wound so mortal
it would extinguish
your last declaration of conciliation.

"PRESCRIBED BURN"

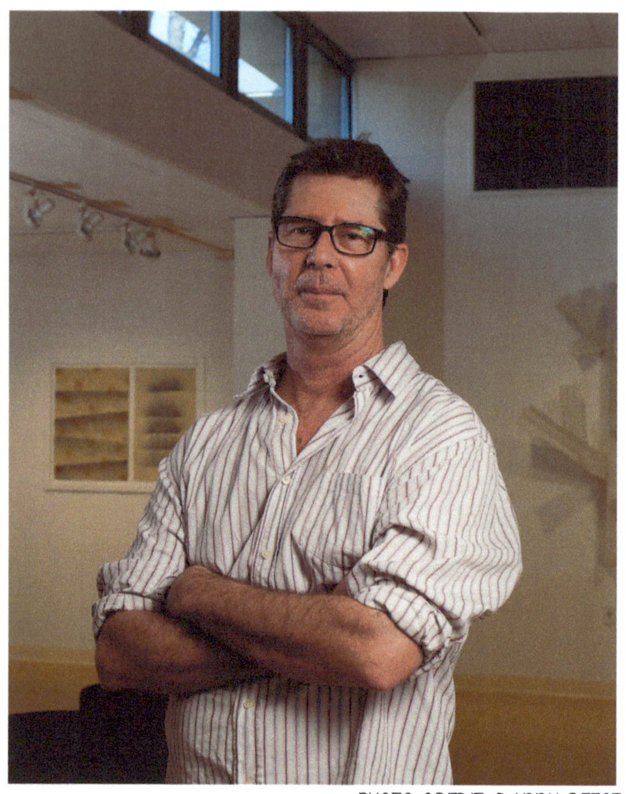

Greg Edmondson was born in Durham, North Carolina. He earned his BFA from the University of Tennessee, Knoxville and MFA from Washington University in St. Louis. He is the recipient of numerous grants and awards including Fulbright and DAAD fellowships to Germany, and residency fellowships to Artpark, the Virginia Center for the Creative Arts, the Santa Fe Art Institute, Black Mountain College and Kuenstlerwerkstatt Munich. "RIVERS and BEASTS", his first book of paintings, was published by Spartan Press in 2017. He may be reached at gregedmondson.net or voegel60@gmail.com.

Hélène Baril is a Parisian based artist. She has exhibited in venues in France, Finland, Switzerland, the United States, Colombia and Poland. She works with various media, including drawing, painting and writing. Her paintings depict fragmented stories inspired by comics and science fiction, associated with her research in situated knowledges and interspecies relationships such as developed in the work of Donna Haraway in the US, Vinciane Despret in Belgium. After starting her career in Finland where she presented her first solo show in 2013 at Äkkigalleria (Jyväskylä), she worked as an artist in residence in numerous places, such as Saint Louis (Paul Artspace, MO, USA) and Medellin (Campos de Gutierrez, Colombia). Her collaborative works have been presented at locations such as WIELS (Brussels), Cooper Union (NYC) and Schloss Solitude (Stuttgart). In Paris, she works with The Cheapest University, a free and experimental artist-run academy.

John Dorsey lives by a river in Southern Missouri. He chose this particular piece to write about because the title spoke to true life events. He is the author of several collections of poetry, including *Teaching the Dead to Sing: The Outlaw's Prayer* (Rose of Sharon Press, 2006), *Sodomy is a City in New Jersey* (American Mettle Books, 2010), *Appalachian Frankenstein* (GTK Press, 2015,) *Being the Fire* (Tangerine Press, 2016) and *Shoot the Messenger* (Red Flag Press, 2017). He is the current Poet Laureate of Belle, MO. He may be reached at archerevans@yahoo.com.

Gina Ferrara lives in New Orleans. She has published three collections of poetry: *Ethereal Avalanche* (Trembling Pillow Press 2009), *Amber Porch Light* (CW Books 2013) and *Fitting the Sixth Finger: Poems Inspired by the Paintings of Marc Chagall* (Aldrich Press 2017). Her work has appeared *The Poetry Ireland Review*, *The Naugatuck Review*, and *Callaloo* among others. She teaches at Delgado Community College and is currently at work on another collection.

Aaron Fine's paintings and drawings have been exhibited widely over the past 20 years. His book of essays and coloring book plates titled "Dialogues on Color" was published by Are Not Books in 2017 and his forthcoming book "Color Theory: a Critical Introduction" will be published by Bloomsbury in 2019. He has been employed by Truman State University for the past 20 years, acting as Gallery Director for most of this period. Currently he is Professor of Art and Chair of the Art Department

Linzi Garcia can be found frolicking through sunflower fields, cemeteries, and bars across the states. Her poetry collection, *Thank You* (Spartan Press 2018), and other poems of hers can be found online, within five anthologies, and in tree nooks near you. Linzi is currently pursuing her master's in English at Emporia State University, where she works as the assistant to the Poet Laureate of Kansas. She is always looking to spend time in new places where she can absorb new poetry, perspective, and whiskey. Please feel free to contact Linzi via linzigarcia@gmail.com.

Jonathan Kline received his MFA in storytelling from the School of the Art Institute of Chicago and has performed throughout the country and abroad. His poems have been published in *Tribes Magazine*, *Big Bridge*, *Yawp*, *Cocktail*, and *The Maple St. Rag*. CDs of his performance monologues include *Conceptual Cowboy Yodeling*, and *Stories My Mother Told Me Never to Tell*. His flash fiction has appeared in the *Maple St. Rag* and the *Xavier Review*.

The Wisdom of Ashes, a short novel, was published by Lavender Ink in 2013. He is currently working on a sequel to *The Wisdom of Ashes*.

Lisa Halley Melching is a photographer, digital artist and educator living and working in her hometown of St. Louis, MO. Her photographic work has appeared in numerous publications and exhibitions over the past two decades.

RC Patterson is a St. Louis resident. He attained a master's in Philosophy from the University of Missouri St. Louis. RC Patterson is an Adjunct professor at Harris-Stowe State University. He has four published books including, *Black Lives Splatter*, *Jim CroMagnon Man*, and *Elegies*. He is an artist, a writer and a teacher.

Nezka Pfeifer is the Museum Curator of the Stephen and Peter Sachs Museum at the Missouri Botanical Garden in St. Louis, where she develops exhibitions interpreting the diverse collections of plant specimens, archival materials, fine art, and biocultural objects belonging to the Garden. Prior to joining the Garden, Nezka has served as curator at several museums where she interpreted collections of taxidermy, art, and ethnographic artifacts for multi-disciplinary exhibitions on a wide variety of subjects (vampires, skateboarding, fairy tales, superheroes, oh my!). She has also worked for historic sites and historic preservation organizations in the Northeast. She thinks the most fun and important part of her job is finding the connections among things and people one would never suspect.

Jeanette Powers is a poet-painter anarchist-queer infatuated with all things working class and non-binary. They have seven full-length books of poetry published, including their latest, *Sparkle Princess vs. Suicidal Phoenix* by Spartan Press, 2018. They live on a river and count John Dorsey and Greg Edmondson as neighbors. They also run the press that put this little ditty of a book into the world. A great believer in community, they also are a founding member of FountainVerse: KC Small Press Poetry Fest and love touring and meeting folks from all over. Find them @novel_cliche or jeanettepowers.com

Ruben Quesada is a contributing editor at Chicago Review of Books. He serves as faculty at The School of the Art Institute, where he teaches poetry writing. His chapbook of poetry and translations, *Revelations*, is available from Sibling Rivalry Press, an inclusive publishing house whose entire catalog is housed in the Library of Congress' Rare Book and Special Collections division.

Stefene Russell is a St. Louis-based poet, writer, and actor. She is also a closet animist, an incorrigible walker and an urban nature lover that values so-called trash trees, weeds and the commonest of birds. Find her at stefenerussell. com, on Instagram (@stefene7), Twitter (@voltarine) and Facebook (facebook.com/voltarine).

Philip Slein is gallery owner and collector born in St. Louis, Missouri, in 1968. In 2003, Slein opened his own gallery on Washington Avenue in downtown St. Louis. Over the past 16 years the Philip Slein Gallery has become one of the most widely known and critically reviewed galleries in the community. Slein is a ravenous collector of art, antiques, modern furniture, advertising, oddities, exquisite timepieces, hi-fidelity, models, and many other things. His downtown loft is a popular showcase of his eclectic collection. His reputation for connoisseurship makes him one of the most sought after figures in collecting in the region.

Brett Lars Underwood is a bartender and a gadabout who writes, promotes and produces happenings and mishaps. His verse and riddles have been published by THE BICYCLE REVIEW, 52nd City, THE SUBTERRANEAN, BAD SHOE, TILL LITERARY MAGAZINE and included in FLOOD STAGE: An Anthology of Saint Louis Poets; The Gasconade Review presents 39 FEET AND RISING and their second edition: MISSOURI IS A GHOST-SHAPED THING. He unleashed SUNLIT INSULT, his first chapbook, in 2011 and ITS BUSH LENT SUBTLE HINTS hit the streets in October, 2013. Spartan Press published his first full-length book of poetry, MUSH, in February, 2018.

Nadia Wolnisty is the editor in chief of ThimbleLitMag.com. Her work has appeared in *Spry, Philosophical Idiot, Apogee, Anti-Heroin Chic, *Isaucoustic, Blue Pepper Review, McNeese Review, Paper & Ink,* and others. She has chapbooks from Cringe-Worthy Poetry Collective, Dancing Girl Press, and from Finishing Line Press and a full-length from Spartan.

AFTER THE FLOOD

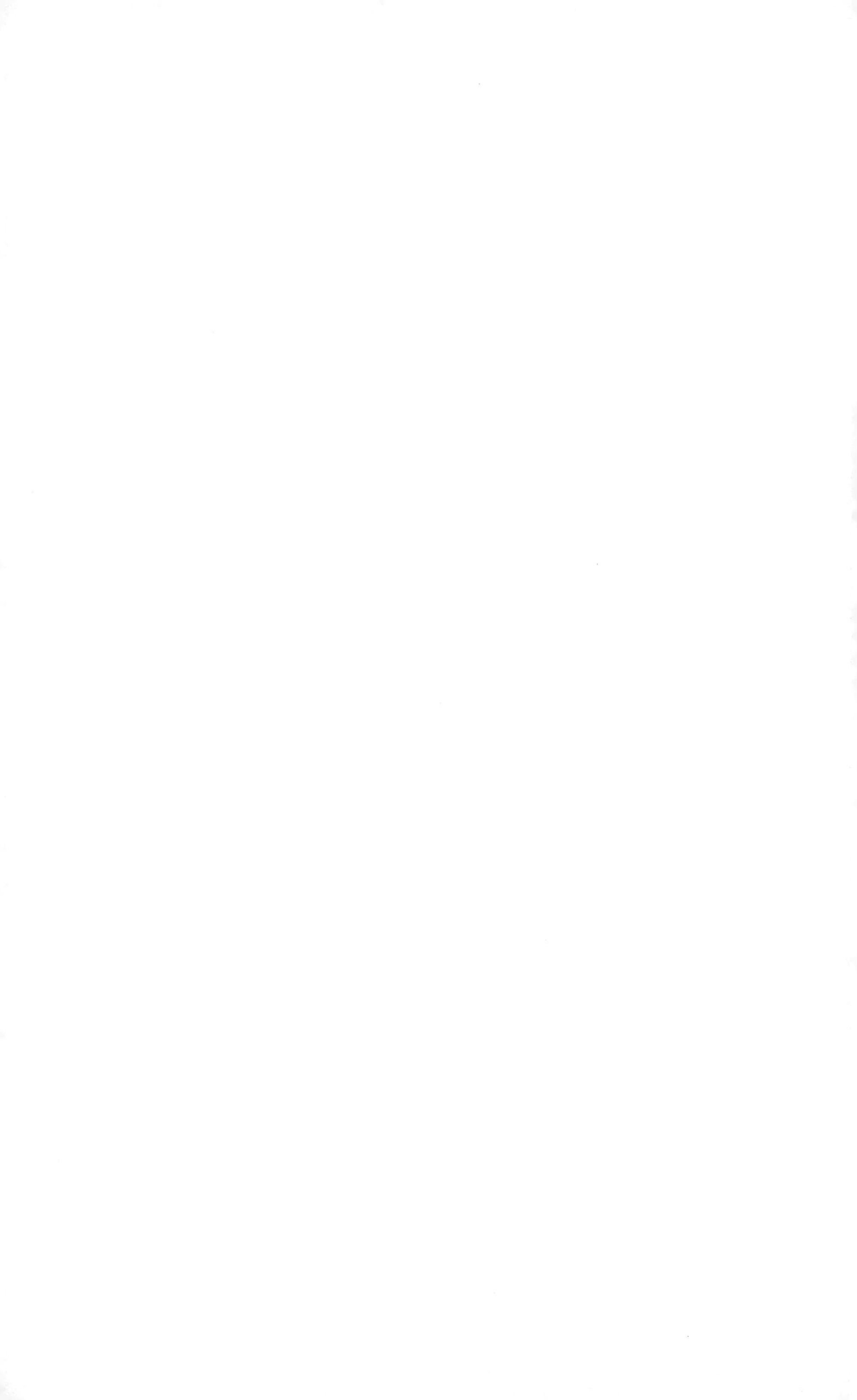